JAZZKEEPERS

A PICTORIAL TRIBUTE AND MEMOIR

To – Rachel –

Keep Vintage Jazz Alive !

Sincerely,

Yuey C. Rure

2/04

JAZZKEEPERS

A PICTORIAL TRIBUTE AND MEMOIR

CLEVELAND, OHIO

(A collection of photographs and conversations with many of
Cleveland's finest jazz performers)

by
GREG L. REESE

PHOTOGRAPHS by RODNEY L. BROWN

COVER DESIGN by ANN WEINBLUM

FOUR-G Publishers, Inc.
1996

FOUR-G Publishers Cataloging-in-Publication

Reese, Greg L.
    Jazzkeepers: a pictorial tribute and memoir, compiled by Greg L. Reese; photographs by Rodney L. Brown ; cover design by Ann Weinblum. Winter Park, FL. : FOUR-G Pub., 1996.

173p. : ill. ; 28 cm.
ISBN: 1-885066-14-7

    1. Jazz musicians--Ohio--Cleveland--Biography. I. Title. II. Brown, Rodney, Photographer

ML 394 .R44 1996

Copies of this book are available from:

Greg L. Reese
P. O. Box 1163
Beachwood, Ohio 44122
(216) 556-3342

and from:

FOUR-G Publishers
P.O. Box 2249
Winter Park, Florida 32790
(407) 679-9331

TABLE OF CONTENTS

DEDICATION

THIS WORK IS DEDICATED TO MY PARENTS
JASPER & MARGARET REESE
AND TO MY GRANDPARENTS
ANNA L. SMITH AND JASPER & ANNIE L. REESE

PREFACE

I am not a jazz critic or historian, but a passionate lover of jazz music and a friend of those who perform the music. My appreciation for the music inspired this work and pays tribute to the many gifted performers who have dedicated their lives to the preservation of this rich tradition in American music. Many fine musicians across the country go unrecognized for their numerous contributions to the musical art form called jazz. They are the true heroes who consistently reinforce the importance of jazz as they perform within communities throughout this nation. Their appreciation and commitment have enabled us to keep vintage jazz a part of American culture and a mainstay in today's contemporary music scene.

An image of a jazz musician captured in the process of creation is truly exhilarating. To freeze a moment that reveals a performing musician's total immersion in the music at a given moment is the intent of this visual essay. Body language, attire, and the shape of various instruments are elements that will enable the reader to feel the mood of each musician. I would like the reader's attention to be drawn to each photo by its visual appeal and not necessarily by recognition of the artist.

This project also affords the opportunity for each musician to express their personal stories, revealing the pains and pleasures of life as a jazz musician.

This is also thank you, a recognition of the countless jazz musicians that continuously dedicate their souls in an effort to keep vintage jazz alive.

Greg L. Reese

FOREWORD

To understand Greg Reese's concern with documenting Cleveland area jazz musicians, you have to understand both his sensitivity and the often overlooked importance of Cleveland jazz to the world. Greg has recognized that in every major city where jazz is being created and played by both new and seasoned enthusiasts, there are brilliant musicians whose contributions will not be heard outside the walls of the clubs where they play. Call it a lack of business awareness, bad luck, or limited ambition -- whatever the case, they will rarely be recorded, never broadcast; yet they will produce music that might equal that of Miles Davis or Duke Ellington. Their contributions deserve recognition beyond the fortunate few who have heard them, and it is because of his respect for this reality that Reese has produced this book.

Separately, few people realize how important Cleveland has been to the jazz world at large. It took less than 20 years for the combination of piano, European marching band instruments, and African rhythm traditions that evolved as New Orleans jazz to move into Cleveland just after World War I. The musicians were segregated back then, color blind when learning, strictly apart when playing, until Cleveland jazz groups integrated in the decade before World War II.

The music was heard everywhere, from the Golden Slipper dance hall to speakeasies and after hours joints. Noble Sissle came from this world, teaming with a formerly obscure ragtime pianist named Eubie Blake to bring the music to Broadway musicals featuring black casts and jazz scores. Art Tatum hung out in Val's in the Alley, and Artie Shaw held forth with his clarinet before leaving the city to start his own band. Guy Lombardo, Woody Herman, Pee Wee Jackson, and numerous other big names honed their genius in their home town. The local talent was so great that Benny Goodman, Duke Ellington, Bix Beiderbecke, and others made certain Cleveland was a regular touring location where they could take the time to jam with the locals.

Each time new styles were invented, Cleveland greats were a part of it. Some labored in obscurity; others, such as Tadd and Caesar Dameron, Freddie Webster, and the like helped create, then hone the 1940s era be-bop before moving to international careers. When the recording of jazz was still in its infancy, Cleveland offered another first through disc jockeys such as WERE's Bill Randle who popularized the music on the radio. Randle would later become famous for helping Elvis Presley and the rock musicians who followed. But his earliest fame come from turning jazz record albums from curiosities for a limited number of buffs into big business that brought jazz into homes where previously it had never been heard.

Today there is a Cleveland jazz renaissance. A growing number of clubs are featuring jazz either on weekends, through Sunday jam sessions, or on what had formerly been off nights. Telarc Records of suburban Beachwood regularly is honored for its recording of top jazz musicians and re-releases of archival material from the early greats. Yet only Greg Reese has taken the time to notice and record what is happening. Through his efforts, the men and women who sometimes perform in obscurity, perhaps influencing others yet seldom being heard themselves, are assured of being remembered. In addition, the greats of the past who have retired to Cleveland, playing locally what they once took to concert halls and clubs throughout the world, will be noted for their careers. And a few of the faces just might become the feted geniuses of tomorrow. Yet all are Cleveland. All are jazz. And all are remembered because of this book.

Ted Schwarz

INTRODUCTION

THE IMPORTANCE OF THE LOCAL JAZZ MUSICIAN

The most important jazz musician of them all is the local jazz artist, especially the elder cats. Charlie Parker, Miles Davis and John Coltrane evolved from these extraordinary individuals who consistently keep jazz popular in communities across the United States. They're the ones that get you ready for New York. You go to New York to get recognition, polish, and a peep at the real story. How well you do depends on how well you've been schooled by the local cats. Most of the famous cats in the New York mainstream come from everywhere but New York. New York provides the finished product and the fire, the local jazz musician provides the awareness and the desire. Without the local cats, there would be no New York jazz scene.

Time and life go by now you're in the mix, experienced, internationally exposed and New York hip. You find yourself going to places you never imagined or either hoped for. The first thing you do when you arrive somewhere new is look for the local jazz musician. He's your ally, he knows where to eat good but cheap. He knows the right cleaners to go to, and he orients you to the elements and environment you are getting ready to deal with.

More time and more life goes by. You've lived your dream. You've played with the greatest and you've played your grandest. Now you step back and analyze all you have sen and done. You're no longer enjoying the hard life of the New York scene. Changes have come about in every way. New York no longer looks the same to you. then it hits, you, you want to go back home. You miss your family, you want to give something back to your community. You're finally ready to truly enjoy life now, so you return to your roots, a 360 degree turnaround. Initially you experience some heavy culture shock, but with what you know to be true and real at this point you make the necessary adjustments. You know you have to go on now you're the local jazz musician and you have to pass your experience and wisdom on to the new crop of young aspiring musicians. Thank god for our local jazz musicians.

Greg Bandy
Drummer Extraordinaire

ACKNOWLEDGMENTS

ALLEN KNOWLES
ANN WEINBLUM
BASIL PHILLIPS
BILL OTT
CECIL RUCKER
DELORES GUYTON
DONALD J. SAGER
DOROTHY BOOKER
GEORGE C. GRANT
E.J. JOSEY
EDDIE BACCUS, SR.
ERNESTINE L. HAWKINS
EVELYN DENNIS
EVELYN SHAEVEL
GREG BANDY
JEWEL HARRIS
JOSEPH V. CUPITO
KATHLEEN HIPPS
LINDA BLOOM
MARCEL ADAMS
MARY LIDERBACH
MICHAEL L. REESE
RICHARD PEERY
RODNEY L. BROWN
ROSS A. COCKFIELD
S.J.MUSE
SIDNEY THOMPSON
TED SCHWARZ
TERRI PONTREMOLI
WILLIAM D. SHOECRAFT

LIST OF JAZZ PERFORMERS

THE JAZZKEEPERS

WELDON "SCHOOLBOY" HAGGINS

"Schoolboy" ran errands and washed glasses for the pimps and gamblers at the Goodtime House where they sold bootleg whiskey out of fruit jars. While working there, he was also responsible for keeping the music going and played plenty of Louis Armstrong's recordings. Armstrong was his early influence and he patterned his style of singing after Louie. His stepfather introduced him to the four-string banjo yuke and he learned to play and sing using various chords.

Charlie Parker hung out at my hotel with his lady when I was with the Ernie Fields Band in Kansas City, MO. Parker was suspended from the union at this particular time due to substance abuse and could only play when the union man left. He and his lady slept in my bed and I slept on the couch. Being with Charlie was like going to the conservatory of music everyday. People loved to be around him, especially musicians.

I played the Sportsman's Club in Covington, Kentucky with Duke Ellington. They had a gig in Cinci, but everybody left Cinci to go over to Covington for gambling and liquor after the set. Sarah Vaughn, Tiny Blackshaw were asked to sit in along with boxing great Ezzard Charles. Charles was not only a great boxer but was an established bass violinist. "Cottontop," a guitar player out of Cinci was asked to sit in along with myself on saxophone. Man we had a jam that night.

Jazz today is like a Rolls Royce will be one hundred years from now. The quality will never decrease.

WELDON "SCHOOLBOY" HAGGINS

CLARENCE "ANDY" ANDERSON

Eighty-four year old Andy Anderson was born in Ontario, Canada. As a child, Andy lived in Oberlin, Ohio but traveled to Cleveland frequently to visit his mother. While in Cleveland, he once visited the Old Hippodrome Theater and saw a performance by the Brown Brothers, a sextet of saxophone players. According to Anderson, the group was *"a regular choir,"* with an alto, tenor, baritone, bass, and double bass saxophones. Patrons who arrived at the Hippodrome before the I o'clock performance only paid a 15 or 16 cents admissions fee.

The Brown Brothers played a number entitled *"The Bullfrog Blues"* that featured the bass saxophone, which had a tremendous impression on young Andy. Andy was hooked on playing the saxophone after seeing this grand performance. At age nine, Andy wanted to own and play the saxophone, but he suffered from an enlargement of the thyroid gland (goiter). Fortunately the goiter was eliminated through prescribed medication.

His family moved to 46th Street between Central and Scovill and Andy attended Kennard Junior High School. He would shine shoes on 49th and Central, hoping to bank enough money to get this much wanted saxophone. One day, following an afternoon of shining shoes, he opened the door to the apartment and found a "C" melody saxophone lying in the middle of the floor. His mother had saved enough money to buy Andy his dream. He remembers picking up the saxophone about noon and by 4 o'clock that same afternoon, he says, *"I was playin' 'Home Sweet Home'."* Andy had never played, or even touched any instrument prior to that glorious afternoon.

When Andy entered Central High School, he joined the orchestra, band and choir. In fact, the entire afternoon was spent in music-related activities -- *"fourth period was band, fifth was orchestra, sixth was music history, seventh was choir and then it was time to go home."* Also, Andy began listening to jazz while he was still in high school. The major source of his exposure to jazz was the drug stores in the community whose owners *"would blast the latest in jazz music"* over the loudspeakers. Anderson says,

(Continued on 2nd page)

CLARENCE "ANDY" ANDERSON

They'd play Bessie Smith, Ethel Waters and the great Louis Armstrong. The introduction to Armstrong's "West End Blues" was so big and heavy that when played it stopped traffic. Louis was young and heavy and blowin' like mad.

During the late 20's and early 30's, such popular stage shows as "Shuffle Along," "Blackbird," and "Butter Beans and Susie" came to Cleveland. They played the Globe Theatre and the Hanna Theatre, which was always a vaudeville theatre. In later years, when the RKO Circuit began, the Palace and the Allen Theater came into prominence.

You also had your dancehalls, you had Zimmermann's on 105th and Euclid, The Dreamland and the Trianon Ballroom. The "big bands" would play these dancehalls and feature bands like Fletcher Henderson, the Mills Brothers and many others.

The Rose Room in the Majestic Hotel was a very popular spot for Black jazz entertainment. All your Black musicians had to stay at the Majestic cause they were not allowed to stay at the other hotels in town.

Eddie Barefield, who had just left Cab Calloway's band was forming a band of his own on the West Coast. He had wanted Don Byas as his "sax man" but I went in Byas' place. This was my introduction to California and the West Coast. I played with Duke Ellington while I was in L.A. Ben Webster took sick and I sat in for him and played with Duke's band for about two weeks. Later, Joe Thomas broke his little finger and I replaced him in the Jimmie Lunceford band. I also did a movie with Louis Armstrong called "Going Places," a movie about race horses. We would sit and relax between shoots and Armstrong would entertain us. He was a very friendly guy. This was around 1939.

Also, while in L.A. I played several "after-hours" spots. They sold bootleg whiskey and the racketeers would have some grand parties at these "after-hours" sets. I remember sittin in one evening with Jimmy Blanton on bass, Billy Strayhorn was on piano and Ben Webster on sax. A little later in the morning, here comes Lester Young, and we jammed 'til the wee hours of the morning. I knew them and they knew me. The respect was across the board.

Coleman Hawkins and Don Byas were my favorites. Coleman made records with Ethel Waters in 1921 on Columbia Records. When he came through Cleveland, he was with Fletcher Henderson just like Lester Young was with Basie. Benny Carter, Buster Bailey, Rex Stewart and Louis Armstrong, you could hear them all at the "after-hours" joint.

White cats could always go up and down on their instrument, because they studied harder. We would learn the "C" scale and start lookin' for a gig playin' "C" scale and would find one. You'd get instruction from the old timers and learn more from swapping gigs.

When I asked Andy if he had any inspiring words for up and coming saxophone players, he responded,

Half the music business is listening. Listen and you will succeed. Players today are not getting the tone quality. They are technically sound, but when I was comin' up, each sax player had his own identity. You could tell Benny Carter from Coleman Hawkins or Lester Young or Ben Webster. Trumpet players were that way too. When "bop" came through and the tenor became real popular, alto players went to tenor and all sax players began to sound alike if you didn't listen very closely.

Andy continues to play clubs and concerts in the Greater Cleveland area.

DAVID FRANKLIN JOHNSON

I started playing guitar at the age of seven. I took private lessons while going to school. I never played guitar while in school; I played lead guitar and bass guitar. I played my first professional gig when I was ten. I played the Majestic Hotel and the Phillis Wheatley during that time. I first hit the road when I was eighteen. I went to Seattle, Washington with a band called The Rays. We were a jazz blues band. After two months in Seattle I got stranded and had to call my parents for money to get a Greyhound bus ticket back to Cleveland. I played with the O'Jays off and on from 1965 to 1970 and also played bass on many of their   recordings. While working the house band at Leo Casino, I played back up for artists such as Stevie Wonder, Little Anthony and Jackie Wilson. I also played with Roy Ayers for three years.

If you got a good guitar from the old days, you better keep it!

DAVID FRANKLIN JOHNSON

KAYE DIANE TRIMBLE

Kaye Trimble began her singing career in church at the age of five. She is a natural tenor but was told by her music instructors that females should not sing in that particular range. Her college voice instructor suggested that she save her money and forget a career in singing because she simply just did not have the talent. Kaye fooled them all and has enjoyed a successful career. Singers that influenced Kaye's style were Billie Holiday and Mahalia Jackson.

Hang in there, Kaye, we love you and think that you are the gifted one!

KAYE DIANE TRIMBLE

BILAL LUMUMBA LIONEL FREEMAN

I started gravitating towards jazz when I was four. I can clearly remember having a plastic white toy trumpet with blue valves. I used to ask my father to play Freddie Hubbard, Lee Morgan and Miles Davis.

I started music theory when I was six. I started out on flute, but that plastic trumpet stayed in my mind. My uncle gave me my first real trumpet at seven. I played all-city orchestra and band through school.

Kenny Garrett is my favorite young alto sax player; he plays like Coltrane. I have a high regard for Roy Hargrove, he plays beyond his years, I like his musicianship. Clifford Brown had a profound effect on me. I was thirteen when I got hip to him. I bought all his albums.

I really like Wynton, he's an extension of the masters. He hasn't reached the level of a Miles or Dizzy, but he is an extension of that. He is a modern day version of them, and has a wide scope in his music. He has covered a lot of ground in his short career.

BILAL LUMUMBA LIONEL FREEMAN

DEBRA K. WELLS

As a young child, my father loved to sing. He also loved the music of Nat King Cole. I used to harmonize with his singing as he did various chores around the house. He was also a great whistler. He used to hold the neighborhood in concert with his whistling while he painted our house. My Dad, George Gaffney, was my early inspiration in many ways. I first sang professionally with Cleveland's own Carl "Ace" Carter. I also performed with Willie Smith and Jesse Dandy, Jr. I was introduced to these fine musicians by jazz enthusiast Sidney Thompson.

I love Billie Holiday. She gave me that strong feeling, that desire and inspiration to sing. I listened to a lot of Stanley Turrentine and Freddie Hubbard. I'd listen to their albums all the time.

Jazz is on the upswing in American society. Kids are getting turned on to jazz and the musicians that perform jazz music. Jazz is an essential art. A lot of music that makes it to the air waves today, so much of it is not original. Jazz is all original. Jazz is an art form created by African Americans and enjoyed universally.

DEBRA K. WELLS

IDRIS ABDUL-LATIF

As a youngster, Idris Abdul-Latif played bongos at political rallies hosted by his aunt. Mongo Santamaria and Big Black are congo players that truly had an impact on Idris's style of play.

Dizzy Gillespie with Chano Pozo introduced the congo to America's straight ahead jazz. Before that, congos were basically played with Latin jazz or Afro-Cuban jazz.

IDRIS ABDUL-LATIF

RUDY MASTRODONATO

MUSA ABDULLAH

BOBBY ENGLISH

TONY HAYNES

CHARLES LASHLEY

SKIP GIBSON

BRIAN BATE

Brass player Brian Bate was asked when he was first introduced to music? He responded,

Before I was born. Really that's the God's truth because me, my sister and brother all heard Mom playing the piano while we were in the womb. She was about 80% deaf but she heard enough to play and play well.

I started out singing, started on the piano at six, trumpet at eight and French horn at eleven. I originally did not want to play the French horn, but it took me a lot of places and did a lot of good things for me. That's what got me into jazz!

The great Freddie Hubbard cornered Brian after playing a gig and screamed, *"Bates! What you tryin' to do playin' two horns at one time?"* Brian responded, *"Well, Freddie, if I could play one like you, I wouldn't have to play two."*

BRIAN BATE

CHARLES PERRY

Charles Perry is a 78 year old jazz vocalist that has been a supporter of jazz for many years.

Wes Columbo, Bing Crosby, Perry Como, anything they sung I could sing, once I heard it. I had like a musical bank. I could sing it. Balladeers was my thing. I liked to hear those guys sing those ballads. But the musicians got tired of me just doing those slow tunes cause they wanted to swing. I can swing but I consider myself a balladeer. Now I swing more than I do ballads. I can tap dance some.

When I was a kid, there was a lot of old hoofers that used to come through the area where we lived. I'd watch them. I learned the time step first and then they showed me a few routines. Next thing I knew, I could tap dance. Yeah, that new fusion that they play, that hard stuff, it has its momentum but the melodic line is so jumbled and so stiff that you can't relax with it. Fusion is confusing.

CHARLES PERRY

RALPH WILLARD JACKSON

My older sisters were musically inclined and my older brother played drums. After my brother went to the service, he left his drums in the basement. My mother and sister encouraged me to pick up the drums and I began to play. I began my practice by trying to play along with records. It gave me self esteem. I'd get on the bus with my drum sticks, but I didn't want people to know that I was a beginner. I wouldn't carry the beginner's book.

Max Roach -- I like the way he was thinking in terms of what he played. Art Blakey always had a good groove. Shadow Wilson was a drummer that the masters respected. My first professional job was in the prison. There were people that I knew in there. Presently, there are quite a few new and upcoming musicians out there. I teach drums and can witness the growing influence by the actions of my students.

I encourage all young drummers to remain focused.

RALPH WILLARD JACKSON

SHIRLEY VERENA COOK

This West Virginia native began singing in the church with her father's sisters. She turned towards jazz after college and has been inspired by singers such as Billie Holiday, Carmen McRae and Abbey Lincoln. Her favorite contemporary jazz vocalist is Cassandra Wilson.

SHIRLEY VERENA COOK

KENNETH ALLEN

Kenneth Allen's uncle turned him onto Dixieland jazz at a very early age. Nat King Cole, when he was with the trio, had a singing style that Kenny found quite inspirational. Eddie Jefferson, King Pleasure and Mark Murphy have truly influenced Kenny's approach to jazz vocals. Kenny also serves as the Master of Ceremonies for many jazz concerts and benefits held in his hometown.

Kenny was asked if jazz was healthy in our society today. His response, *"Yes, jazz is healthy in American society today, but it will never exist as it did in the past."*

KENNETH ALLEN

ROBERT L. HARRIS

"Horn players today want to play 90 miles per hour, they got to learn to slow down and appreciate the quality of the music." So says, Bobby Harris, who decided that he wanted to play the saxophone after hearing the sound of the great Dexter Gordon. While living in New York City, Jackie McLean had a studio and gave free music lessons to whoever wanted to learn absolutely free. This is where Bobby met Sonny Fortune, Sonny Red, Joe Henderson and Ernie Watts. According to Harris, *"Many of today's artists are making loads of money by revamping tunes established by the jazz masters."*

Bobby was asked what brand name horn was his favorite. *"There are several quality horns out there on the market, but the mouthpiece and the reed play an extremely important part in determining the performance of the instrument."*

Bobby's sons and daughters are all very musically inclined. *"My children listened to jazz while they were still in the cradle. They went to sleep listening to Charlie Parker, John Coltrane and many other jazz masters."*

ROBERT L. HARRIS

JUDITH "JUDY" STRAUSS

Both of Judy Strauss's parents played piano. Her mother was a piano teacher and taught her for about six months until she began private lessons from a classical instructor who would come to her home. Strauss says a turning point for her occurred when she was in high school. *"I got interested in jazz through hearing some of the records my older brother played around the house, then I took jazz lessons."*

Dave Brubeck, Hampton Hawes, Oscar Peterson, Red Garland, Les McCann and Ramsey Lewis are artists that Judy admired as a young jazz pianist.

Marian McPartland, records by Bess Bonnier, Barbara Carroll and Diana Krall were some of the female jazz pianist that I studied. In 1975 I played on a bill with Shirley Scott, Stanley Turrentine and Donald Byrd. In 1985 with Ray Brown and Dizzy Gillespie.

It is so important to get the younger people introduced to jazz. There are a fair amount of clubs to go to hear it, but the prices that they pay the musicians have not improved in the last thirty years although the drinks and food have gone up. Concerts -- in order to see the big names you have to go to concerts. The tickets get to be fairly costly.

Jazz is listened to by only 8% of the population, so it's a fairly small part of the market but it is also the same with classical, two specialized kinds of music that you have to develop a taste for.

We do a program called "A Musical Journey in Jazz" since 1982. We have done this program about 50 times at schools, neighborhood centers and malls. The purpose is to increase the knowledge of the general student body about other cultures and the introduction of jazz to the students at an early age.

JUDITH "JUDY" STRAUSS

RAYMOND ARTHUR ODOM

We had a piano at our home and I became interested in playing it at the age of three. I remember at the age of five I went to my first concert at Severance Hall. When I returned from the concert, I was able to play most of the concert for my Mother because I was able to remember much of what I heard.

Besides piano and keyboards, I also play guitar, trumpet, saxophone, flute, clarinet and piccolo. My woodwind major was bassoon. I've played violin and at one time I was first chair violinist for the Philiss Wheatly Orchestra.

Jazz grabs your emotions, it sits you down, it relaxes you as you kinda get lost in what's going on within the music. Jazz tends to work as a soothing antidote when confronted with the difficulties of life. It truly seems to have that sort of effect on individuals.

RAYMOND ARTHUR ODOM

HOWARD ALPHONSO SMITH

I'm from Fayetteville, Tennessee, 15 miles from Alabama and 25 miles out of Huntsville and 82 miles south of Nashville. I started music in church and I left home when I was about 14 or 15. The lady next door during the Second World War gave me a trombone and a lady down the street gave me a trumpet. We had a piano in the house and everybody in my family took piano lessons.

I could play piano by ear. I could play anything that I could hear. My ear "thang" was so good, and I learned so fast. Music was the only thing that could make me sit in the house for a couple of hours at a time. I remember the first piano solo that I did in church. It was a song called "I Have Changed My Life For Jesus." I graduated from high school in '51. After I got out the service I studied voice and secondary piano.

When I was incarcerated, that's when I really got into music. I studied the trombone, played in the band. That was my job. We had a 72-piece band and a 17-piece orchestra and a small combo. On Monday and Wednesday you studied composition and arranging and music history. After I got out, I got a job as head doorman at the country club in 1962.

I highly respected the sound of Billy Eckstein and later on Nancy Wilson. Jimmy Rushing, they called him Mr. 5X5, with the Count Basie Band was also a favorite. But I always tried to do things my way.

HOWARD ALPHONSO SMITH

JACK I. SINGLETON

After being discharged from the service, Jack traded a camera for his first set of drums.

It was a mismatched set, Man, everybody was on the poor side back then.

Jack played the tom tom drum in kindergarten and later played throughout his career in the Armed Forces. He played the service clubs and any other time he got the opportunity to play. He was a show drummer, but his heart was always with jazz. His favorite drummers are Jimmy Cobb, Art Blakey and Philly Joe Jones.

Jazz is well and alive but will never be as great as it was during the late 40's and early 50's.

JACK I. SINGLETON

CECIL WILLIAM RUCKER, JR.

My instrument is called the vibraphone, vibraharp or vibe. I studied as a drummer from the age of twelve, went to music school and also participated in the school band and the Elks Club. In 1974 while continuing my study of drums in college, I met and heard the great Roy Ayers. Roy promised to give me some pointers if I switched from drums to vibes and I did just that! I called several music stores lookin' for a deal on a used set of vibes. Once I located a set, I got a loan and picked up the vibes the same day!

I truly admire Roy Ayers, Lionel Hampton. Hampton -- I saw him play the drums and the vibes at the same time. It blew me away. There's Milt Jackson, Bobby Hutcherson -- those cats are outstanding.

I'd like to see clubs across the country feature jazz at least five nights a week. Younger musicians need more opportunity to develop their skill in front of live audiences.

CECIL WILLIAM RUCKER, JR.

DOLORES SMITH

Dolores Smith began singing jazz professionally in the mid-sixties.

I've tried very hard not to pattern my singing style after anyone. I am pretty much self taught, yet I learned to breathe from Johnny Mathis. I also like Sarah, Carmen and Ella, Abbey Lincoln, I love Abbey!

When she was asked about the state of jazz in America today, Delores makes this observation:

We have lost a great number of the masters and I have not seen anything replacing them. Too few of our new and young vocalists are aware of the talent of a Sammy Davis, Jr. He was an excellent vocalist but was not allowed to be a vocalist. He was allowed or accepted as an overall performer. If Sammy had been allowed to perform as a vocalist, Frank Sinatra would have had to take a back seat. The man was incredible.

DOLORES SMITH

JIMMY BOYD

ROY VALENTI

JOE PEARSON

JOSEPH MALINOSKI

MIKE ALEXANDER

"HOOFER"

ED FERGUSON

ROBERT LOCKWOOD, JR.

KENNY BURRELL

BENNY BAILEY

PERRY WILLIAMS,III

CHARLES PERRY, 1952

"SCHOOLBOY" & "ACE"

CARL "ACE" CARTER

LLOYD PEARSON

TERRANCE "EASY QUIS" QUISENBERRY

C-C BIRMINGHAM

EDDIE C. BACCUS

I'm from Lawndale, North Carolina about 48 miles from Charlotte. I heard an album by Errol Garner. He was the first pianist that I liked. When I went to the school for the blind is when I got the opportunity to play piano. We couldn't afford a piano of our own. In 1955 I heard Jimmy Smith and I was fascinated because I never heard an organ played like what he was doing. From then on, I liked the organ also.

No keyboard can compare with the quality of a B-3 or C-3 Hammond organ. I can remember playing jobs. We'd play six or seven days a week and we had to move the big organ at least five or six times a week.

I did travel for awhile. I played with Ike Cole and Tony Lovano. We had a trio. Ike is Nat Cole's brother and Tony is Joey Lovano's father.

EDDIE C. BACCUS

RAYMOND MILLER

I was always fascinated with the guitar. I took up the guitar during my last days in high school around 1945.

Charlie Christian -- he was the daddy of everything. Then there was Barney Chessle -- he was top notch. Wes Montgomery turned everybody around. There will never be another Wes.

RAYMOND MILLER

JESSE DANDY, JR.

I was introduced to music at Scott Elementary School in Birmingham, Alabama (Pratt City). I was a trumpet player, the only instrument they had in the music room was a trumpet. I continued playing trumpet through high school. I lived in the band room. I participated in the marching band, the orchestra, the whole bit.

I went to Alabama A&M after high school and continued to play trumpet. Eventually, I was president of the marching and concert bands while in college. I went into the Air Force (Strategic Air Command) after leaving Alabama A&M. They sent me to Great Falls, Montana. I would work eight hours a day but it was so cold in Great Falls that you stayed inside about 80% of the time. I'd go over to the Airman's Club and there was a bass sitting in the corner. I cleaned it off and began to pick it up and pluck.

This was my first introduction to the bass. It became a ritual -- I'd get off work, go to the Airman's Club and practice four or five hours through the evening. I had no formal training. After practice, I would go home and play some Miles and listen to bassist Paul Chambers. I'd try to imitate his playing style and I got pretty good at it. Eventually, I ended up playing with a trio at the Holiday Inn in Great Falls. I met Duke Ellington in Great Falls.

I have found that many people refer to jazz as the devil's music. But it's not the devil's music, it's God's creation. God made us to create this music called jazz. Jazz is therapeutic, it's healthy for you, it makes you feel good inside. The person playing and the person listening both experience the same pleasure.

When Jesse was asked about great bassists today, he immediately gave the names of Ron Carter, Ray Brown and Christian McBride.

JESSE DANDY, JR.

RHODA MARIE CASSELL

Rhoda Cassell is an extraordinary jazz vocalist who listened to and appreciated instrumental jazz before she developed a love for vocals. In 1968, her rendition of "Loverman" won her first place in a "jazz in the park" contest judged by the great Lionel Hampton. In 1972, she turned from jazz to gospel and traveled the United States with a gospel troupe known as the "Voices of Living Sound."

In 1981, she moved to New York City as a full time jazz vocalist and worked with greats such as Carter Jefferson, Ron Burton and James Spaulding.

Upcoming young jazz vocalists must be committed. I recommend that they move to New York City if possible. In my opinion, New York is still the jazz capital of the world.

Carmen McRae, Billie Holiday and Betty Carter are Rhoda's favorites.

RHODA MARIE CASSELL

SAM BLACKSHAW

Jazz organist Sam Blackshaw learned the keyboard in an attempt to improve his singing ability. Sam was a singer with a local singing group before he became interested in the organ. He stopped in a club one evening and filled in for a jazz organist who failed to show up for a gig. He knew the tunes and chord changes as a result of his singing experience and became the club's organist for the next six months. Sam has been playing the organ continuously since that night at the club.

While working the chittlin' switch circuit, Sam has performed with jazz greats George Benson, Sonny Stitt, and Grover Washington, Jr. His style of play has been influenced by brother Jack McDuff, Jimmy Smith and Richard "Grooves" Holmes.

When asked to compare the electronic keyboard to the Hammond B-3 organ, Sam replied, *"There is no comparison, It's like matching a Volkswagen to a Rolls Royce."*

SAM BLACKSHAW

JOHN K. RICHMOND

This Chicago native, John Richmond, started playing violin when he was ten; at the age of thirteen he discovered jazz; by the age of 15 he had a clarinet; and at the age of seventeen, he joined the navy and went to the Naval School of Music in Washington, D.C.

I used to go to the movies, my brother was an usher and he could get me in free, I thought it was a big deal. There was a movie with horrible acting and a terrible plot. It was the Benny Goodman story. The music was great, so all the other stuff didn't matter. And in the band on screen was Stan Getz, Buck Clayton, Lionel Hampton and Teddy Wilson and that was it! I walked out of the theater singing some of those Fletcher Henderson arrangements that Benny Goodman played and I never looked back. My musical tastes went forward and backward from that point.

A clarinetist that absolutely knocks me out is Buddy DeFranco. I can't even pretend to play the way Buddy does.

My all time favorite jazz person is the great Duke Ellington.

JOHN K. RICHMOND

MAR'SHAL JEAN BAXTER-BECKLEY

My mother was a gospel singer and we -- myself, my sister and my brother, the first three children -- were her background singers. I was about three or four at the time and we were called the Thomas Singers. That was my mother's maiden name. At fourteen, I was doing R&B and a little jazz. I made my first recording at age fourteen. The name of the tunes were "I'll Never Be Free" and "Any Old Way."

Ella Fitzgerald was one of the first people that truly impressed me. (Between her and Dinah Washington because my aunt was Dinah's best friend). They went to school together in St. Louis. Dinah would visit my aunt's house and she taught me how to sing "What A Difference A Day Makes." Betty Carter is also one of my favorites.

I've shared the stage with Gladys Knight, Dionne Warwick and Mavis Staples. My ex-husband played with the O'Jays and I traveled with them for sixteen years. We were always at the Apollo Theater. I met Redd Foxx, Slappy White and shot marbles with the Jackson Five.

Contemporary vocalists such as Dianna Reeves -- this girl is excellent, Diane Schuur and Nancy Wilson are my favorites. I tell my vocal students to learn your skill well from the ground floor up. Always be sure of yourself. Musicians love that. And never try to sound like other people. Everybody has their own voice and they should use it.

MAR'SHAL JEAN BAXTER-BECKLEY

GERALD W. LINTHICOME
"BUTCH"

My Mother called me "Putts" and the guys I played with thought "Putts" was "Butch." They started calling me "Butch" and it's gone on for all these years.

I started playin' the "C" melody. It was almost as big as me. I was about eleven or twelve. I got a lot of my training while I was in the school band in junior high school. My mother got a deal on a brand new King Zephyr alto sax for about eighty five dollars. That's when I switched over to alto.

Johnny Hodges just knocked me out, Man, with that beauty. Benny Carter, Eddie "Cleanhead" Vincent played alto and sung the blues. I once saw him perform and Bud Powell was on piano. Bud was about seventeen playin' that piano. I used to play for tap dancers, shake dancers and blues singers. It was a great experience playin' for tap dancers.

I think jazz is on the rise. The jazz clubs are few and far between but the concert scene is beginning to develop. Jazz is being taught in colleges by jazz musicians. Cats comin' out of college and playin' like mad. I hear these young-sters, these young guys play, Man, and they play very well. They are all over their horn, excellent technique, but the one thing that they don't have is that mellowness. Everybody is in a hurry.

GERALD W. LINTHICOME
"BUTCH"

EDWARD JULIUS WASHINGTON, JR.

Eddie Washingon became interested in the drums at age five by first playing the bongo drum using wooden rulers for sticks. His dad used to play recordings of Count Basie and Duke Ellington and he was always fascinated by the drumming.

He played drums in his high school band and began to pay close attention to the drumming styles of Max Roach, Art Blakey and Buddy Rich. His uncle, Jacktown, also a fine jazz drummer , turned him on to his very first gig traveling on the road.

EDWARD JULIUS WASHINGTON, JR.

EDDIE CLEOPHAS BACCUS, JR.

This twenty-five year old rising star, Eddie Baccus, Jr., has a lot to say and play. *"I went to Berklee College of Music in Boston, I learned more from my friends than I actually did from the school. I really miss it a lot."*

Eddie was asked who were some of the masters that influenced him over the years. *"Definitely Parker, Stitt, Trane and Ammons. I can't leave out Sonny Rollins and Miles and Joe Lovano. He's one of my favorite cats, Joe Henderson."*

I have a variety of sounds, I have to push myself harder. I practice maybe a half an hour or hour a week which is pretty bad. I remember a time that I practiced fourteen hours a day. I'm going to get back on that kind of regimen. I was playin' the club one night and saw a cat in the audience, it was Lester Bowie. Lester called me about six months later and said, "I got a couple of dates for you, New York, Rome and Japan.

Eddie Baccus, Jr. is certainly on his way to stardom. He is a fine young saxophonist that should be an inspiration to all young and upcoming musicians.

EDDIE CLEOPHAS BACCUS, JR.

JANET L. MOORE

Janet Moore loves the singing styles of Dinah Washington, Billie Holiday, Nancy Wilson and Anita Baker.

I enjoy singing the song "No Regrets." It sheds light on a lot of things that have happened to musicians personally. We have no regrets, we keep on movin' on."

JANET L. MOORE

JOE BELLINI

JACKIE "O"

NEAL CREQUE

DON BANKS

J. T. LYNCH

EDDIE WOODS

BOB FERRAZZA

BILLY HADDON

EUGENE JONES

GERI ALLEN

TONY BYRD

"SKEETS" ROSS & LAMAR GAINES

KEVIN MUHAMMAD

BOBBY WATSON

DEWEY JEFFRIES

CYNTHIA WOODARD

ERNIE KRIVDA

I was introduced to music almost immediately. My father is a musician, a jazz saxophone player. Music was always there. I can remember vividly hearing the recordings of Coleman Hawkins, Roy Eldridge, the Count Basie Band and Benny Goodman at an early age. I started playing clarinet when I was seven. I wanted to play tenor sax, but the clarinet was considered the starter instrument of the reed family. I started playing gigs for bucks in the seventh and eighth grades. I played in polka bands and did several commercial gigs through high school. I was playing both the clarinet and alto sax at that time.

My first year in college I got a call to play with the Jimmy Dorsey Band. I left college to join the band, the solo tenor chair. This was my first truly significant gig. I've played and recorded with the Quincy Jones Band back in the 70's and also played with the Grooves Holmes Band. I've played opposite Herbie Hancock, Cannonball Adderley and many others while working the Smiling Dog here in Cleveland.

Don Byas, Coleman Hawkins, Lester Young, Stan Getz, Zoot Simms, Gene Ammons and Cannonball are musicians that have inspired my playing. Cannonball was responsible for me getting the Quincy Jones gig. We became pretty good friends.

Jazz is more of an accepted part of the fabric of American life. It's not playing the role it once did in the '30's and '40's, but it is playing a greater role than it did in the '60's and '70's. Hopefully, jazz will maintain its level and popularity. I don't believe that it's going away.

ERNIE KRIVDA

ROBERT NATHANIEL ROSS
"SKEETS"

When I was two years of age, my cousins nicknamed me that because I couldn't pronounce the word mosquito. It went from Skeeter to Skeets."

I'm from Chattanooga, Tennessee. My mother played piano. We had an old upright piano in our home when I was born. I was bangin' on the piano at the age of two and at the age of eight I began to take lessons, fifty cents a week. Playing piano became my hobby; the piano was my toy. We didn't have too many toys during those times. I found great consolation playing the piano.

Nat Cole was my idol after Count Basie. Count was easy to hear and playing his stuff was rather simple. I learned to emulate him. Duke Ellington was a little too heavy for me, I had to grow into Duke. Bud Powell was really playin', playin' and thinkin'. I had never heard a piano player like Bud. I still liked Nat, but Bud had something different and it brought me into my own. I was schooled tryin' to study Bud. Also George Shearing -- I was learning how to improvise, to dig within the chords.

Pianos have their own personalities just like people. The tone and action are very important. I like a piano that rings brilliant on the upper end and one that sounds like thunder at the lower end. You find that quality in the Steinway and Baldwin pianos. I am not a feathery pianist. I play heavy, so I am emotional and I believe in dynamics like Oscar Peterson, highs and lows.

ROBERT NATHANIEL ROSS
"SKEETS"

WILLIAM "BILLY" BLACKSHAW

There was a hot tamale place, the real hot tamales, and I remember a barber shop, with the peppermint thang that goes around. But right across the street my uncle was playin' cocktail drums. When I saw him playin' that day, it really knocked me out. I was head over hills for drums from that day on.

When I first got my drums, they were from the Salvation Army. I was twenty-one. I was ridiculous. I think the drums saved me from the streets. All I did from morning-noon-'til night was practice playin' the drums. Cats was goin' out partyin' and I was in the basement, I had records and I was playin' drums. I'd practice so hard that my father would whip me some nights and I'd sneak back down to the basement and start playin' again. I had no real idols at that time.

WILLIAM "BILLY" BLACKSHAW

JOHNNY "DUCK" MCCALL

Johnny boxed in the gloves in the early 1960's and acquired the nickname "Duck". *"If they didn't see the right hand, that's what they had to do!"*

Little Jimmy Scott gave Johnny his first professional gig in 1953. He later was called by Zola Taylor (female member of the Platters) to join them in California for a spell.

The great Jackie Wilson was an inspiration to "Duck" McCall. McCall sings first tenor and can pull the house down at the drop of a hat.

JOHNNY "DUCK" MCCALL

MELVIN WAYNE BURKS

In the 7th grade, man, we joined the school band. We joined hoping to see some honeys. We joined 'cause we knew girls were goin' to be there. A cat named Robert Crawford was playin' cornet and it sounded good to me. I wanted to play, and that was it.

In the twelfth grade, Chuck Magione was hot around that time and Tom Brown's Jamaican Funk. We used to do that number in every talent show. After I went to school I was into Wynton, Clark Terry and Terence Blanchard. I didn't care for Miles and Coltrane at that time. Afterwards, it was like a growing process, like reading literature. You start off reading "Dick and Jane." Then, you begin reading books on the level of the Bible. It just grew after I began listening to the masters.

Jazz is the only American form of music. There's nothing phony about it.

MELVIN WAYNE BURKS

JOSEPH JEROME SAUNDERS

Oscar Peterson, Ahmad Jamal, McCoy Tyner, Herbie Hancock, Keith Garrett, Chick Corea and Cecil Taylor are the core of pianists that I truly admired and have had an impact on my playing.

The Steinway and the Mason-Hamlin are my favorite pianos. The action on the Mason-Hamlin may not be as liquid as the Steinway, yet they both are melodically superb. The Yamaha has recently improved and is also a quality instrument.

I feel that there is a renaissance of jazz, but this is not a jazz era. I just think the industry is pushing some young and brighter talent that is coming along. They are technically very astute, but jazz to me was also a lifestyle, an intellectual movement.

Cyrus Chestnutt, Jacky Terrasson and Stephen Scott are a few of the newer talents that Jerome feels are making a significant impact on the contemporary jazz scene.

JOSEPH JEROME SAUNDERS

CLEVELAND'S OWN
GREG BANDY

A drummer of exceptional skill and imagination, Greg Bandy received his initial training in Cleveland, Ohio. Moving to New York, he began his professional career under the guidance and management of Roy Ayers and Myrna Williams, and soon found himself in demand, performing with such established jazz stars as Joe Henderson, Jackie McLean, Roy Ayers, Betty Carter, Pharoah Sanders, Leon Thomas, Little Jimmy Scott, and Yusef Lateef.

Greatly in demand as a teacher, Greg conducted jazz clinics at Oberlin Conservatory (1981-1985), Cleveland State University (1981), and the Universities of Massachusetts and Edmonton (1980). He taught at New York City's Joseph P. Kennedy Center, and at Mind-Builders Creative Arts Center, in the Bronx. In 1982 he was voted Jazz Musician of the Year by the *Cleveland Plain Dealer.*

Bandy's scope is wide, his versatility ranging from scoring for the Ruth Williams Dance Company and a professional play, "Their Eyes Were Watching God", at Cleveland's Karamu House Theater, to an acting part in 1985 Metropolitan Opera production of "Porgy and Bess" at Lincoln Center. He also appeared in the Negro Ensemble Company's 1990 production of "Sidewinder," a play based on the life of trumpeter Lee Morgan.

He has been seen in documentary films featuring singers Betty Carter and Little Jimmy Scott, and appeared on the TV show, "A Man Called Hawk," playing and recording with Valerie Simpson. As a model, Bandy took part in a photo session with Brooke Shields for Modern Bride magazine. Skillful at setting bodies in motion, Greg Bandy has also accompanied such well-known dancers as Debbie Allen, the Copasetics, and Tina Pratt. He is truly a drummer extraordinaire.

I started playing drums when I was seven; my father inspired me to want to play. My Father was a music promoter here in Cleveland in the 50's and 60's, and that's how I got a chance to see a lot of great musicians as a kid. I ended up playin' with many of the cats that I met as a kid later on. My Father wasn't a jazz musician but I think he always wanted to be.

(Contined on 2nd page)

GREG BANDY

I got my first drum set when I was eleven or twelve, a three piece cymbal and a hightop, Jacktown style. At nine I began my studies at the Cleveland Music School Settlement. I continued to play through high school. I was in the marching band, concert band and jazz band at Glenville High School. I studied with one of the major percussionists with the Cleveland Symphony Orchestra, Mr. Rob Matson, until I was fifteen or sixteen. My high school music teacher, Mr. James Turner, really turned me around musically, he pulled my coat! While at Glenville High, I was a member of the Glenville Jazz Ensemble. We were guests on the Don Robertson Show, a TV show on Channel 25 back in the 60's. We played the show and David Frost was one of Mr. Robertson's guests. This was before Frost had his own talk show. Robertson was so impressed with us that we performed every Wednesday on his show for quite some time.

I began playing the Cleveland club scene when I was about thirteen. My father's friend, Reggie Red, was a tenor sax player and he got a job from my father. The gig was at Cleveland's Bricklayers Hall. As an extension of appreciation to my father, Red hired me as his drummer and from that time on I began to play with cats around the Cleveland area.

I tried to go to Baldwin Wallace College for a minute but it didn't work out. After finding out that I wasn't interested in college, that's when I decided to go to New York and pursue a career as a jazz musician.

When I went to New York, I had my own band. We were called Black On Black. We got to New York, hooked up a pad, and the great Herbie Hancock was my neighbor. Herbie lived in apartment 3D, I was in 7D with the band and Joe Newman lived up above me in 8D. Yes, Riverside Drive, 202 Riverside Drive, that was my first pad in the Big Apple.

Everybody in my band came back to Cleveland, but I stayed. I began to meet all kinds of people. In New York, you had to learn about the music. The school room is one thing, but the stuff you learn just living there, seeing it, playin' it, being a part of it, liking it, sleeping it, can't be replaced. New York was the real school. I had to go to New York and just bite the bullet.

Bandy was asked if he encountered any difficult times in the beginning during his time in New York. He laughed,

In the beginning, the middle and the end. It goes in and out. You can be hot one day, like a firecracker, then out the next. You got a million cats up there, that's what makes you tough. Guys are just lookin', waitin' for you to make a mistake so they can get a shot. Or sometimes they come see you if they heard that you might be good. They come lookin' for you.

Stateside, I played with Arthur Prysock, Betty Carter, Freddie Hubbard, Stanley Turrentine, Lionel Hampton, George Benson, Abbey Lincoln, Jackie McClean. Jackie raised me. Eventually I began to freelance. I got away from the band concept. I played with a lot of organ players.

A lot of people that play drums feel like you have to bang them. If you can finesse the drums you stand a better chance of working. I love everybody, but Roy Haynes, Art Blakey and Elvin Jones caught my eye way down the line. Me and Haynes are tight. I let him use my drums while he played a gig here in Cleveland. We are both Pisces. I met Haynes about my third week in New York and met Charlie Mingus my first week along with Betty Carter. I met them all at the same club. They were just sitting around having a drink. I grabbed some sweet connections my first week in New York. I've traveled to a ton of countries in Europe, all of Japan, Africa, South America, the Caribbean, Canada, Mexico, Spain and others. Thinking of New York, my birthday party is a classic in Harlem. They call me the Mayor of Harlem. Just recently I finished a gig in Stockholm and thought I'd stop by New York and check the block. I know everybody from the pauper to the State Building.

In New York, jazz came from uptown. Those who rewrite jazz history indicate that jazz was downtown around the village, but it came from uptown. Remember that! Harlem was where the action was. I remember one night, me, Jack McDuff and Lonnie Smith were going to make a double organ album. We used this club for a rehearsal and finished jammin' around four o'clock in the morning. As the owner was gettin' ready to lock up and pull the shades (cause it's four o'clock) there's a knock on the door. They open the shade and the door and here comes Stanley Turrentine. He'd been downtown and he stopped by because he wanted some real stuff. He said, "Y'all got to do another one," so we jumped back on the bandstand with Turrentine and played for another hour. Then there was another knock on the door and this time it was George Benson. We went back to the stage and we finally came off at about 7:30 in the morning and the place was packed. The people were hoopin' and hollerin'. That's what I dig about New York.

Greg Bandy presently resides in Cleveland. He still travels quite extensively but you can catch him performing at many of the local clubs and concert locations.

KENNETH E. LEEGRAND

My grandfather was a drummer who played behind some pretty big acts. There was always jazz and blues being played throughout our house and I became interested in the saxophone at the age of three or four. I started on the clarinet during school and I gained a wealth of classical experience. I began playing sax in junior high school. I participated in the jazz band at Kirk Middle School in East Cleveland.

My first professional gig was at a place on St. Clair called Martin's Lounge. I was playing baritone sax and clarinet. Musicians that have inspired my style of playing have been John Coltrane, Charlie Parker, James Moody and Dexter Gordon. I have shared the stage with the great Freddie Hubbard, Dexter Gordon and Joe Sample.

Jazz has become the predominant music taking over classical music in our schools. Jazz seems to immediately grasp the student's interest and that is not to take anything away from classical music. I love it!

Jazz players are not compensated monetarily as rock 'n roll and R&B players. That's the way it is. Those who are true to the art are usually the ones who don't get paid.

KENNETH E. LEEGRAND

RONALD DAVIS

Ron Davis, who began singing after being a musician says, *"I played trombone and trumpet before I discovered that I had singing abilities. Etta James, Coco Taylor, Lou Rawls, Joe Williams and Arthur Prysock are individuals that I studied to develop my own style."*

RONALD DAVIS

WILLARD "BILLY" GRINAGE, JR.

When I began to concentrate on jazz, I heard a recording by Clifford Brown and that was it! Lee Morgan, Freddie Hubbard, Joe Gordon, Miles, Dizzy, Roy Eldridge were my early influences.

Billy was asked to render an opinion about the abilities of today's new or younger jazz artists.

Most younger cats had the opportunity to study at an early age and learned how to do everything the right way. This accounts for their fantastic technique, the mechanical handling of the instrument. Terrence Blanchard, Nick Peyton and of course Wynton are superb.

I sincerely wish that there was more unity amongst jazz musicians. Local musicians are fragmented, very independent in their approach to the art. It would be very helpful if the musicians would come together. The result would be that the music would have a stronger foothold in today's music scene. That's why my band is called "Unity of Sound".

WILLARD "BILLY" GRINAGE, JR.

DEBRA STEWART

Debbie Stewart, from Mobile, Alabama, was not aware of her unique singing ability until a group of established musicians encouraged her to seriously consider singing professionally. This was in 1986 and Debbie has established a very solid career as a jazz vocalist.

Her early influences have been Nancy Wilson and Aretha Franklin. She reveals that such standards as *"'Old Folks' and 'My Foolish Heart' are my all time favorites. I truly enjoy performing both of those songs."*

When asked who was her favorite contemporary vocalist, she responded, *"The young R&B vocalist Brandy. She catches my heart. She's got that old amen corner sister sound goin' and it knocks me out."*

DEBRA STEWART

ISMAIL DOUGLAS

HAL WYANT

C-C BIRMINGHAM & JACKIE "O"

BOBBY HUTCHERSON

GEORGE CALABRESSE

JACKIE WARREN

LARRY GLOVER

LAMAR GAINES

RALPH BROWN

LARRY SHARP

MATT GOLD

PAT HARRIS

NAN O'MALLEY

ABDULLAH MAGHRIB

JAZZ GREATS:
BILLY ARTIST, CELIL RUCKER, RAY MILLER, BILLY BRADSHAW & BILLY HADDON

DON SPEARS

MATTHEW "CHINK" STEVENSON

Matthew Stevenson picked up the name "Chink" from his buddies during childhood. Stevenson, who was pudgy as a youngster with high cheek bones and somewhat tilted or slanted eyes, was called "Chink" by his young buddies and the name has been with him ever since. *"My buddies said I looked like a Chinaman, I could not shake that nickname and I am still called "Chink" today."*

Stevenson, a superb acoustic bass player, began his career as a saxophonist and switched to the bass in 1957 after serving in the U.S. Military. Stevenson had formal training but gained most of his experience while traveling and playing gigs across the United States.

Ray Brown is the cat that truly influenced my style of play. I rate him at the very top of the list when we speak of jazz masters. There is also Percy Heath, Buster Williams, Leroy Vinegar and Charlie Mingus.

When asked about today's young and upcoming bass players, Stevenson feels that the young Christian McBride is the leader of the pack.

MATTHEW "CHINK" STEVENSON

KAMAL ABDUL ALIM

Unfortunately, because of the marketing process of the recording companies, they're not marketing any new music. The younger musicians are playing the music that was played in the 60's. As far as innovative music, they're not really coming up with it. Yet, I have a lot of respect for some of the younger musicians, Roy Hargrove, Terrance Blanchard. They got a bunch of them. They comin' out so fast. They are great technically equipped musicians, but because of their age and experience, they tend to follow in the shadows of what has been previously created rather than being innovative.

KAMAL ABDUL ALIM

MARVIN CABELL

This Chicago native, Marvin Cabell, was initiated into jazz when he was quite young.

I had my own band when I was ten. At an early age, I was inspired by Illinois Jacquet, Sonny Stitt and Bird. I started playing professionally when I was ten, we were getting paid for small gigs so we were professional.

Marvin has been a very successful tenor sax player for many years but recently began playing the lyricon. About his career he says,

Fingering on the lyricon is a combination of the flute, sax and clarinet. It's an electronic wind instrument with a reed. I've worked with George Benson, recorded with Lonnie Liston Smith, Ron Carter, Billy Cobham and Johnny Lytle. I played tenor and flute.

Jazz is stalled! The schools, the musicians, the younger cats sound the same. There is very little creativity. They use the same tonal concept. You turn on the radio and it's difficult to distinguish one artist from another.

MARVIN CABELL

GIROD GILLISPIE

Jazz has always been healthy within our society. It is the rule of the black experience. It rotates around all forms of music. Without the jazz, we wouldn't have the music. Jazz is a part of the way of life.

GIROD GILLISPIE

ARCHIE MCELRATH

At the age of four, Archie McElrath sang in the church choir. In elementary school, his music teacher noticed his ability and enrolled him in music class. After high school, he joined the USO, traveled to Europe and began to sing professionally. He later moved to New York City and met Chuck Magione who encouraged him to seriously pursue a career as a jazz vocalist.

McElrath patterned the singing styles of Johnny Hartman and Joe Williams; yet he is a tenor. A male singing in the upper register was something that McElrath had to feel comfortable with. To sing in the upper register and have voice control was the key to his success. Johnny Mathis became his principal influence. Archie also loves the sounds of Morgana King and Cleo Laine.

ARCHIE MCELRATH

JOSEPH DEJARNETTE, JR.

I'm from Praco, Alabama in Jefferson County. My Grandfather, who was a music instructor, bought me my first trumpet. I had an instructor from Florida A&M and William Simpson, whose brother played in Count Basie's orchestra, were very instrumental in my development. I was very young. After entering the military, I played in the orchestra with the 173rd Military Band.

The truth about jazz is that it supersedes the technical skills that you have -- you have to get inside the music. I have had the pleasure of playing with Duke Ellington, Cannonball Adderley, Art Blakey and Houston Pearson.

JOSEPH DEJARNETTE, JR.

JAZZKEEPERS

CLUBS, ORGANIZATIONS & INSTITUTIONS

JAZZKEEPERS

NATIVE SON
15305 KINSMAN ROAD

NIGHTTOWN
12383 CEDAR ROAD

UP TOWNE GRILLE
11312 EUCLID AVENUE

TRI-C JAZZFEST
Cuyahoga Community College

"The Tri-C Jazzfest" was initiated in May, 1980 as a two-day event featuring student clinics, jazz performances at the Cuyahoga Community College Metro Campus as well as two evening concerts at the Palace Theatre in Cleveland's Playhouse Square. Since 1980, "Jazzfest" has grown in size and scope. It is now an eleven-day event with ancillary programming presented throughout the year.

"Jazzfest" was founded with the following goals:

1. To provide an educational opportunity for students and people of all ages and backgrounds to further their abilities, understanding and appreciation for jazz;

2. To increase public awareness and appreciation for jazz as a significant American art form;

3. To preserve the history and foster the development of this unique music; and

4. To bring world-class jazz performers to Cleveland audiences.

These goals inform the programming philosophy, which is in turn reflective of the diverse needs of the community and the artform.

Jazzfest attendance for live events and educational activities ranges from 40 - 44,000. An additional 200,000 persons hear live and delayed broadcasts aired on WCPN, Cleveland's National Public Radio affiliate.

160

TRI-C JAZZFEST
2900 COMMUNITY COLLEGE AVEUNE
CUYAHOGA COMMUNITY COLLEGE

CLUB ISABELLA
2025 UNIVERSITY HOSPITALS DR.
UNIVERSITY CIRCLE

EAST CLEVELAND PUBLIC LIBRARY
14101 EUCLID AVENUE

SIXTH STREET UNDER
1266 W. 6TH ST.

NORTHEAST OHIO JAZZ SOCIETY

The Northeast Ohio Jazz Society has become the major jazz service organization in northeastern Ohio. The NOJS is in the forefront of jazz programming and education. The NOJS has taken a leading role in presenting jazz programs for children at Beck Center, the Cleveland Children's Museum, the Cleveland Music School Settlement, and many schools.

The NOJS provides many services to its more than 900 members, ranging from discounts on tickets for jazz events, discounts on jazz magazine subscriptions, and an award-winning newsletter, *Jazz Central*. The NOJS also provides a voice to Ohio jazz musicians through its musician's Liaison Committee. Monthly "Pub Nights" provide members with a chance for socializing while supporting the vital northeast Ohio jazz club scene.

The NOJS has received funding from the Cleveland and George Gund Foundations, the National Endowment for the Arts, the Ohio Arts Council, and the Lila Wallace-Reader's Digest National Jazz Network.

The NOJS is governed by an elected Board of Trustees. Its work is carried out by many hard working volunteers.

ST. MARK'S PRESBYTERIAN CHURCH
1319 EAST BLVD.

MARDI GRAS SPORTS BAR
1423 EAST 21ST STREET

MR. Z'S RESTAURANT
3312 W 117TH STREET

LANCER'S BAR & LOUNGE
7707 CARNEGIE AVENUE

BOARDING HOUSE RESTAURANT & JAZZ CLUB
11311 EUCLID AVENUE

THAT PLACE ON BELLFLOWER
11401 BELLFLOWER ROAD
UNIVERSITY CIRCLE

THE CLEVELAND BOP STOP
BRADLEY BUILDING
WEST 6TH & LAKESIDE

NAME INDEX
TO PERSONS AND PLACES
IN
JAZZKEEPERS